Y0-DFH-161

A GIFT FOR:

FROM:

Copyright © 2016 Hallmark Licensing, LLC

Published by Hallmark Gift Books,
a division of Hallmark Cards, Inc.,
Kansas City, MO 64141
Visit us on the Web at Hallmark.com.

All rights reserved. No part of this publication
may be reproduced, transmitted, or stored in
any form or by any means without the prior
written permission of the publisher.

Editorial Director: Theresa Trinder
Editor: Kara Goodier
Art Director: Chris Opheim
Designer: Brian Pilachowski
Production Designer: Dan Horton

ISBN: 978-1-63059-856-3
BOK1534

Made in China
0617

THANK YOU for YOUR LESSON

By JEANNIE HUND

Hallmark

A MESSAGE OF THANKS TO TEACHERS, COACHES, MENTORS, AND OTHER MOTIVATORS

Caring about other people and contributing to their well-being is powerful, important stuff. In fact, it may be the most important thing we do as humans.

You are someone outstanding who lives each day with this in mind, someone whose amazing smarts and generous heart make our world a better place. You gladly go the extra mile to mentor, coach, counsel, or teach, and for that . . .

I WANT TO

THANK YOU.

THANK YOU
FOR BEING
a person
WHO
TO HELP
BE

LIVES
OTHERS
THEIR BEST...

AND FOR

LOOKING

W

AND

at the
ORLD
SEEING
WHAT IS
POSSIBLE.

YOU DEVOTE
TO RECO
PEOPLE'S
AND BUILDING

YOURSELF
GNIZING
STRENGTHS.
ON THEM.

YOU SAW SOMETHING IN ME—

SOMETHING
OF PROMISE,
of value—

AND YOU TAUGHT ME

TO **SHINE.**

Thank you FOR ENCOURAGING ME

TO DO MY BEST, to give MY ALL . . .

AND TO FIND OUT HOW

AMA

ZING

THAT FEELS.

YOU BRING OUT

CHAM

MY INNER
...PION...

AND YOU MAKE ME WANT *to do* BETTER,

to be BETTER,
EVERY
SINGLE DAY.

THANK YOU
AND FOR
celebr
EVERY SINGLE
PAINFUL STEP

OR HAVING MY BACK.

ating,

MY IMPROVEMENT

JOYFUL,

OF THE WAY.

EVEN WHEN I STUMBLED, YOU ASSURED ME

THAT EVERYONE STUMBLES ...

AND YOU TAUGHT ME
ONE STEP
TO KEEP

AT A TIME,
ON GOING.

Thank you FOR BEI

EVING
IN ME.

EVEN WHEN I DIDN'T FEEL
TO DREAM
BIG

LIKE IT, YOU ENCOURAGED ME

AND TO GIVE 100%.

THANK YOU FOR

BIG

WHEN

SHOWING UP —TIME I TRULY NEEDED A BOOST—

› FOR NOT LETTING ‹
DISCOURAGEMENT
GET THE

BEST OF ME,

FOR NEVER
QUITTING

&

NEVER LETTING ME QUIT ON MYSELF.

THANK YOU

FOR INSPIRING

me.

YOU GUIDED ME

WITH WISDOM, PATIENCE & WARMTH...

AND YOU'RE
THAT TRUE
IS IN THE
THAT IT'S
ON THE

MINDED ME SUCCESS TRYING— MEASURED INSIDE.

THANK YOU

FOR KNOWING EXACTLY WHEN TO STEP IN.

YOU SENSED
WHEN I WAS
HOLDING MY OWN
AND WHEN
I'D HIT
A WA

BUT YOU UNDERSTOOD THAT STRUGGLE IS A PART OF

NATURAL GROWTH.

THANK YOU FOR CHEERING ME ON,

FOR CHALLENGING ME—

AND FOR KNOWING

just how much to **PUSH.**

THANK YOU FOR THE heart AND soul

THE HOPES AND DREAMS...

THE INNER *fire* YOU

LIT

IN ME.

THANK YOU
FOR BEING AN
EXCEPTIONAL
PERSON

WHO HELPED ME BECOME A BETTER ME.

THANK YOU

If you have enjoyed this book
or it has touched your life in some way,
we would love to hear from you.

Please write a review at Hallmark.com,
e-mail us at booknotes@hallmark.com,
or send your comments to:

Hallmark Book Feedback
P.O. Box 419034
Mail Drop 100
Kansas City, MO 64141